FLOODGATES

FLOODGATES

Discovering the Treasure Within You

ELISABETH JOHNSON

Printed in the United States of America

Publisher's Cataloging-in-Publication data
Johnson, Elisabeth.
Floodgates : Discovering the Treasure in You / Elisabeth Johnson
ISBN -13: 978-0-692-05177-1
1. Tithing   2. Revelation.

Book Cover Design by Townsend Solutions, LLC

Author Photographs by Tree of Life Photography

While the author has made every effort to provide accurate Internet addresses at the time of publication, neither the publisher nor the author assumes any responsibility for errors or changes that occur after publication.

First Edition

Acknowledgements

I am most overwhelmed by this part of the book! There are so many to thank!

I will begin with my Pastors Errol and Jennifer Davis, thank you for your covering and your impartation of faith. Thank you for seeing in me what my Father sees and giving me the grace to grow.

Vicki thank you for your words of affirmation and encouragement to pursue writing.

To everyone, my family, my friends, my church family, my co-workers who showered me with encouragement and affirmed my Kingdom value. A special thanks to Nancy, Angie, Toya.

To my sisters, Rachel you will never know how much I value you. Because of the flow of your floodgate, I desired more. Candace, thank you for challenging me and pushing me to greater faith, you inspire me. Kym, thank you for your encouragement. To my brother, Anthony, I praise God for you and I value you.

To my parents, Pastor Darryl and Lady Gloria Jones. When I truly think about the intentionality and precision of the plans God has for me as your daughter my heart is filled with gratitude and thanksgiving. There is a true gift of word of wisdom that flows from your gates! I am eternally grateful and completely biased that my Father has given me the very BEST! I could not ask for a more authentic display of what it means to walk with Him.

To my children, Elisha, Nehemiah, Josiah and Gabriel. May the Lord woo you into a intimate relationship with Him.

To my husband, Adrian, thank you for your vision and protection. I thank God for my union with you. There is no one else I would rather walk through life with.

Contents

Preface

Like the first time you fell in love or when you got *that* toy you really wanted for Christmas, but didn't think your parents could afford, moments such as these forever imprint your mind and heart. There are such moments in my life when the Holy Spirit has literally intervened, imprinting my heart and mind, disrupting my normalcy, and changing my perspective forever. These moments have been the beginning of a deeper revelation of who God is and the abundance He desires to provide for me. One such moment, I remember well. Something in me was awakening. I didn't know what it was but I was tired, frustrated, and grieved. I couldn't even tell you why I was feeling such strong emotions; but they were sending me over the edge. I felt as if I was always on the brink of bursting into tears. I was tired of the "same ol' same ol'."

I remember waking up one morning and asking the Lord, "Is this it? Is this all there is?" I was bored with going to church. I was frustrated because I didn't know what to do. And if there was more, I didn't know how to get there. It was a Saturday morning, my husband and I were preparing to go to a marriage conference at our church. He didn't want to go, which frustrated me even more. But nonetheless he went with me. The men and women separated for one of the sessions. The speaker began to go off on what seemed like a tangent. I don't know how the presentation shifted from marriage and relationships to true worship. Not only was there a shift in what the speaker was saying, but I noticed a shift in the atmosphere. The presence of God was permeating the atmosphere like I had never felt before. I really didn't completely understand what was going on, but I was captivated and I wanted to understand more of what God desired from me as a worshiper. Inspired, I bought the workbook on worship. I left the workshop that afternoon with a sense of heaviness.

Sunday morning I woke up and even though I had a glimpse of what true worship was supposed to be in the life of the believer, I still felt a sense of frustration and a lingering heaviness. I retrieved the workbook out of desperation and proceeded to do a study from John chapter 4. The woman at the well. Jesus says, "You worship what you do not know, but there is coming a time when the true worshipers will worship in spirit and in truth." This stuck with me. Honestly, I don't remember the sermon but I had a divine appointment waiting for me. In our Sunday school class, the lesson was from John 4. The woman at the well! *Did He hear me?* After the lesson, a wonderful woman of God began to share her story with the class. For some reason her honesty and transparency touched my heart. I approached her after Sunday school ended and thanked her for sharing her testimony. I was so grateful to her. Somehow the room cleared quickly and it was only my sister, this woman of God, and me in the room. She embraced me. All of a sudden it was like a flood. All that heaviness I had been feeling overflowed. There was a great release of God's presence all over me. I was consumed and overwhelmed with the love of God in a way that I had never experienced before and it was real! From that day forward my worship, my prayer life was never the same! I had been cleansed and freed at the same time.

I do not impose my personal experiences of God's manifested presence in my life onto others. Everyone is unique and our Father knows how to reach each one of us in those unique ways. But I do believe that there should come a time (or hopefully many times) in each one of our lives that we consider, "Is this it? Is this all there is?" My prayer for you is that the Lord spark a greater desire in your heart and spirit to move toward the abundant life that was prescribed especially for you. That you would discover the treasure that our Father has imparted to you and for you. That you would walk in mind transforming revelation that will overflow into every area of your life and spill into the lives of those around you.

Introduction

Before we begin I want you to know that we are going to look at the most familiar set of scriptures regarding tithing. In studying these scriptures this is what the Lord told me;

You tend to study the scriptures from an earthly perspective....meaning you already know that My word speaks to your earthly situation. And for you mature believers, you know how My word is the power and the backbone behind the word you speak. You know that life and death are in the power of the tongue. You know that you can speak things which be not as though they were. So you come at My word in a position that is looking up...and that's good... it is good to look toward the hills where your help comes from. BUT I challenge you to study the scriptures from a heavenly perspective. I raised you up with, my Son, Christ, and seated you with him in the heavenly realms. Therefore, if you are seated with Christ in heaven then you need to study scriptures top down....you need to recognize your spiritual position. The perspective changes from looking up to looking down...

The Lord said to me, *"Instead of asking,*

Introduction

'What can I receive from heaven to work in the earth?' I need you to ask this as you study, 'What can I pour out of heaven into the earth?'"

This is how we will look at Malachi 3:8-10 (KJV)....top down.

Will a man rob God? Yet ye have robbed me. But ye say, Wherein have we robbed thee? In tithes and offerings. Ye are cursed with a curse: for ye have robbed me, even this whole nation. Bring ye all the tithes into the storehouse, that there may be meat in mine house, and prove me now herewith, saith the Lord of hosts, if I will not open you the windows of heaven, and pour you out a blessing, that there shall not be room enough to receive it."

My hope is that we look at tithing with a new perspective...more than just money or provision and more than an act of worship but as a key to insight and revelation.

Part One

The Storehouse: Revelation Revoked

By the word of the Lord the heavens were made, and all their host by the breath of his mouth. He gathered the waters of the sea as in a bottle; he put the deeps in storehouses.

Psalm 33:6-7 (NRSB)

The Storehouse: Revelation Revoked

The key to any kingdom principle can be found in the beginning. I am fascinated with the relationship between the Old and the New Testaments. The Old Testament is the establishment of the new and the New Testament is the evidence of the old. Therefore, within Genesis lies three important references for understanding the word of God: God's original design and intent in the earth, the destructive effects of sin in severing the fellowship between the Father and His beloved and the constant struggle to re-enter into fellowship with God the Father.

1

The Original Design and Intent

"In the beginning God created the heaven and the earth. And the earth was without form, and void; and darkness was upon the face of the deep. And the Spirit of God moved upon the face of the waters." Genesis 1:1-2 (KJV)

The earth was without form. Formless has a few definitions according to the

The Original Design and Intent

Merriam-Webster dictionary:

>1. having no regular form or shape

>2. lacking order or arrangement

But I think the last definition is the best contextual fit:

>3. having no physical existence

The earth had no *physical* existence because God had not yet spoke. As soon as God begins to speak, that which was formless began to take shape; it began to manifest. The NASB says, "and darkness was over the surface of the deep," Some versions say, "deep waters." Anything that God has not yet called is in darkness, it is covered, it is hidden, it is a mystery, it is unrevealed. As the Spirit of God moves upon the face of the waters, the light of God uncovers that which is hidden in the depths. As God's Spirit moves over the waters, His light is so brilliant, so illuminating, God sees that which is hidden in darkness....and He begins to call it forth into being. "He reveals mysteries from the darkness and brings the deep darkness into light" (Job 12:22, NASB).

Whatever God calls forth from darkness comes into His light. He sees it...He calls it...it forms. This is our first insight to the process of revelation.

But you are not like that, for you are

a chosen people. You are royal

priests, a holy nation, God's very own possession. As a result, you can show others the goodness of God, for he called you out of the darkness into his wonderful light.

-1 Peter 2:10, NLT

God diagnoses the urgent need for light in the earth. Therefore, it is the first element He speaks into physical existence. "And God said, Let there be light: and there was light. And God saw the light, that it was good, and God divided the light from the darkness" (Gen. 1:3-4 KJV).

Proceeding light, God continues to call and speak the heavens and the earth into existence. He fills the earth with plants, trees, fruit, and animals. Then He plants a garden in the midst of four rivers, and this is where He places man. He places man in the best spot in Eden. Provision is made in every way. Every demand is supplied, every need is met, every desire is fulfilled. The storehouse is complete. Man does not have to "work by the sweat of his brow." Exhaustion and fatigue are not in the equation. There is no need for sweat equity. God has made his work easy. However, the provision is not without conditions.

The Lord God took the man and put

him in the garden of Eden to till it

and eat of every tree of the garden;

but of the tree of the knowledge of
good and evil you shall not eat, for
in the day that you eat of it you
shall die.

- Gen. 2:15-17, NRSV

The intent is in the design. In creation
God provides everything man needs to work
successfully in the garden. Jehovah Jireh
provides physical needs: water, plants to
eat, companionship. He provides man with
purpose; He gives man dominion and
rulership over the earth. And He provides

man with His Spirit and likeness," And God said, Let us make man in our image, after our likeness: and let them have dominion over the fish of the sea, and over the fowl of the air, and over the cattle, and over all the earth, and over every creeping thing that creeps on the earth" (Gen 1:26 KJV).

"And the LORD God formed man *of* the dust of the ground, and breathed into his nostrils the breath of life; and man became a living soul" (Gen 2:7, KJV). The intent is in the design. Eden is the first earthly storehouse. I wondered, why did God make Eden first then man? Why didn't

He make man first? God says, *"Because I created man in a satisfied state. I didn't want man to get caught up in what I could do, what I could create. I wanted man to look at creation, marvel at what I had already done and adore Me. I wanted him to see Me as Jehovah Jireh... God who has already provided."* He provided *first, then* made man. He already fulfilled every provision for you before you were created! From the beginning He set up man to live eternally in abundant provision... eternally in purpose and eternally in the His presence. This is God's original intent toward us.

2

The Fellowship of the Father and His Beloved

I'm not sure what it is about "daddy" coming home from work, but when I was a young child I remember looking forward to my father coming home. My children are so excited when my husband comes home for dinner each night. As soon as they hear the garage door, they run to the door and yell, "daddy!' even when it's just me closing the garage door after throwing something in the recycling bin. They are thrilled when he takes a day off of work to stay home and spend time with them. They just want to be around him, they just want to be in his presence. But can you imagine the heartbreak of a father who comes home expecting his children to run to him saying his name, "daddy, daddy!" as he enters the door only to find that no one comes to greet him? They are all hiding in their rooms consumed with *something else*.

And they heard the sound of the Lord God walking in the garden in the cool of the day, and Adam and his wife hid themselves from the presence of the Lord God among the trees of the garden. Then the Lord God called to Adam and said to him, "Where *are* you?" So he said, "I heard Your voice in the garden, and I was afraid because I was naked; and I hid myself"

- Gen. 3:8-10, NKJV

That something else is sin! God is and always will be our pursuer, before sin and after sin. The heartbreaking part is that when Adam sinned, the love he had for his Father was replaced with fear. He is always seeking us out, looking for us to enjoy His presence without fear.

> Such love has no fear, because perfect love expels all fear. If we are afraid, it is for fear of punishment, and this shows that we have not fully experienced his perfect love.

> -1 John 4:18, NLT

Adam lost his perfection. He lost the capability to experience His perfect love.

Floodgates

The word beloved means a person who is greatly loved. Now like any Father, God comes up with the ultimate plan to get us to the point of knowing *we* are His beloved:

How do I demonstrate my love for them in such a way they will be perfected in love? What can I do to take us back to our relationship we had when we used to walk together? How can I pursue my beloved in such a way that he experiences my love?

First, he will have to die. This is the only way I can separate his spirit being from his physical being, which is now tainted with sin. Second, he will need to need Me so he will have

The Fellowship of the Father and His Beloved

"to work by the sweat of his brow." It must become difficult so he will recognize his need for Me.

Provision will become difficult. Worship will become difficult. God develops a plan to satisfy both the need for provision and worship...

So in the meantime until his spirit returns to Me, while man is still living in the earth, something or someone has to die to meet the requirements of provision and worship.

3

The Struggle

I remember tug of war as a kid. Two teams pulling in opposite directions. The team that won, won based on several variables; the number of people on the team, the strength of each individual, and the strategies of the individuals.

The tension between good and evil is

in a constant tugging motion. A choice always has to be made. The fruit reappears in our hand each time we are faced with a temptation. We have to choose everyday, every minute if we will give in and bite. It would appear that the enemy would have every advantage over us. He *seems* stronger, the number of temptations *seem* to outnumber our will, and the strategies he has developed after observing humanity since the fall of man is vindictive and calculating. It *seems* like we can't win. But it's all a matter of perspective.

There is a strong interdependent

relationship between provision and worship. Out of the provision of God flows worship, when we truly worship God, He provides. It takes us back to the first storehouse, Eden, where every provision was met. God would take Adam for walks through the storehouse. Together they would look and marvel at all God had created. On these walks God points out everything created, every provision made. "*See* I have given you dominion over the fish of the sea and over the birds of the air and over every living thing that moves upon the earth...every plant yielding seed that is upon the face of all the earth, and every tree with seed in its fruit; you shall have them for food" (Gen. 1:21,26, NRSV). Together they would admire everything God had done, everything God made and agree that it was "indeed very good." This is worship! A lifestyle of agreeing with God. The more you agree with Him ...the more He reveals to you!... And the more "good" you see!

Once Adam ate the fruit from the tree of good and evil his eyes were opened. Opened to what? Well, if we go back to the walks God and Adam would take together before the fal l , when God's spirit and Adam's spirit were one, God would show Adam something. Adam would then see as God saw, from the Father's perspective. Then Adam would agree that it was good. But since Adam's eyes were opened, he could now see from a different perspective. His perspective was split, the perspective of good *and* the perspective of evil. Adam could now acknowledge something he didn't or couldn't acknowledge before. Acknowledge doesn't just mean "to know something," it means to recognize as a fact or truth; to declare one's belief in. Adam's ability to recognize fact or truth had been compromised. As a perfect being, Adam only recognized God's word as the fact or truth. Now he had the capability not only to recognize the good God had provided (worship) but he could also recognize the evil Satan presented. He traded the truth for a lie, good for evil, provision for poverty, intimacy for enmity, blessing for a curse, unity for discord. It was a bad deal. So now, back in the garden, before the fall of man, provision was made and worship was easy; after the fall provision is labor intensive and worship requires sacrifice.

Then to Adam He said, "Because you have listened to the voice of your wife, and have eaten from the tree about which I commanded you, saying, 'You shall not eat from it'; Cursed is the ground because of you; In toil you will eat of it, All the days of your life. "Both thorns and thistles it shall grow for you; And you will eat the plants of the field; By the sweat of your face. You will eat bread, Till you return to the ground, Because from it you were taken; For you are dust, And to dust you shall return."

The Struggle

-Gen. 3:17-19, NASB

Now it's a struggle. And the struggle is made apparent in the next generation.

Now Abel kept flocks, and Cain worked the soil. In the course of time Cain brought some of the fruits of the soil as an offering to the Lord. And Abel also brought an offering— fat portions from some of the firstborn of his flock. The Lord looked with favor on Abel and his offering, but on Cain and his offering he did not look with favor. So Cain was very angry, and his face was   downcast.

- Gen. 4:2-5, NIV

The act of worship toward God is to recognize and give reverence for the provision He has given. Because sin fractured the fellowship of God and man, due to the impurities that lie in the heart, God must test the clarity of the heart. Because He is holy it is against His nature, His very being, to be in the presence of anything tainted. Abel gave his very best to the Lord, while Cain brought *some* of the fruits of the soil as an offering to the Lord.

The Struggle

Abel brought the firstborn of his flock. God was pleased with Abel's act of worship but displeased with Cain's. Cain then kills his brother and God says, "What have you done? Now you are under a curse and driven from the ground...When you work the ground, it will no longer yield its crops for you. You will be a restless wanderer on the earth." Cain says, "My punishment is more than I can bear. Today you are driving me from the land, and I will be hidden from your presence;" (Gen. 4:10-14, NIV).

Wait a minute...God did not say

anything about him being hidden from his presence.... God said, "you are under a curse"... Cain understood that in being cut off from the land, he was being cut off from provision. He also understood that not being in the presence of the Lord is the worst part of the curse. What he cannot bear is being cut off from the presence of the Lord. Worship is interrupted when giving does not flow freely from the heart.

The good news is that if we pick God on our team and allow His strength to work in us, He alone is so much greater than anything or anyone on the opposing team.

The Struggle

He makes a way to restore what was lost...

our provision, our worship, our perspective.

Part Two

The Storehouse: Revelation Restored

I was chosen to explain to everyone this mysterious plan that God, the Creator of all things, had kept secret from the beginning. God's purpose in all this was to use the church to display his wisdom in its rich variety to all the unseen rulers and authorities in the heavenly places. This was his eternal plan, which he carried out through Christ Jesus our Lord.

Ephesians 3: 9-10, NLT

The Storehouse: Revelation Restored

Now that we understand God's original design and intent and the struggle that was birthed through sin which caused the revocation of our access to the storehouse, our focus can shift to the Father's pursuit to re-establish storehouse provision for His beloved. God is ever pursuing us to restore that which was lost. In His plan of restoration, He makes covenant with us in order to bless us, mature us, invest in us and pour out of us.

4

A Covenant Blessing

In Genesis 12, God calls Abram and he says, "I will make your name great and you will be a blessing. I will bless those who bless you and whoever curses you I will curse, and all peoples on earth will be blessed through you" (NIV).

In chapter 14, after Abram recovers his nephew and his goods, King Melchizedek of Salem who is a priest of God Most High blesses Abram. In response he gives the Man of God *a tenth* of everything recovered... this should put your mind to ease about your tithe money going to the Man of God. Side note: If you are leery of how your tithe money is spent then prayerfully consider a new church home where you can get under leadership you love and trust...giving will be easy. We will discuss this further in chapter 6.

Then Genesis chapter 15 begins like this ... "After these things the word of the Lord came to Abram in a vision." Notice how Abram went from *hearing* the word of God to *seeing* the word of God. The less he held back from God the more his revelation increased. We know this because Abraham is our example of one of the greatest sacrificers in the bible, besides God himself. He was willing to sacrifice the very gift God had given him. The very gift that had been prophesied *three times*. First a *spoken* word, then a *visionary* word, then the *Lord appeared* to Abram and said, "I am God Almighty; walk before me, and be blameless. And I will make my covenant between me and you, and will make *you* exceedingly numerous" (NRSV). God is restoring the abundance lost in the garden. The NASB says this, "And I will multiply *you* exceedingly." Put a pin in this one, this will be a key point in the benefits of revelation.

5

The Maturation Process

Children are self-centered by nature and you will find that self-centeredness is the root of immaturity. This is why parents have to intentionally teach their children to share and give. Picture two children. Both have their grip on the same toy. Mine. Mine. Mine!

My husband and I have been blessed

with four beautiful children. My oldest was two and a half when our twin boys were born. Whew! Those were some tough years that developed our patience. The last one snuck in five years later. We had just made it to a point when our oldest three were semi-independent. No more potty training, they can make their own sandwiches, they were all in school; but with a new baby coming we were back to square one. In a sense, I had nearly forgotten about how terrible the twos were. But I found myself there once again, trying to reason with a two year old that had no reasoning skills. So many times I would have something to give him, but because he couldn't see it, in his young mind, he assumed that I would not give him what he wanted or needed. And no matter how I tried to tell him or show him "I have what you want. I have what you need." He was already in such a tantrum mode, too disappointed, too upset to see what I had waiting for him, he was unable to let go of what appeared to be a disappointment to receive the treat I truly had in store for him.

As adults, we too, can get stuck in tantrum mode, unwilling to let go of what we think we know instead of trusting the heart of our Father. I will never forget. It was another one of those moments. I was sitting in the driver's seat of my car about to run an errand. My husband and I had just finished *Financial Peace University* and I was toying with this idea of discontinuing the use of my one and only credit card. I felt the Lord daring me to trust Him more. *Is it really that deep, Lord?* And I said these words, "Lord, if you want me to give this up, I will be giving up plan B, my emergency plan, my 'I want to buy it now and I'll pay later convenience' ...show me a sign." Two weeks later my credit card bill came and I realized the credit card company had penalized me with a late charge of $30. In the eight years I had had the credit card I don't think I had any late payments. I noticed the credit card company had changed the date of payment. The deadline had been moved up. *Ok, Lord, I see you.* And that was my cue. I shared my prayer with my husband and we both agreed we would take a step of faith and cut up the credit card. We would no longer use credit as a resource. Within seven months, on a modest middle class household income we paid off $30,000. It's been nine years since we have used a credit card. I truly believe that once we let go of what the world said we needed and had to have, He showed us a greater way. It might not be about the use of credit cards but there is something in all our lives we cannot see yet. Some area in our life where the Lord is daring us to trust Him *more.*

Many of us face the same dilemma and have similar inner conversations with ourselves regarding tithing. We can't see what our Father truly has for us. We are too busy holding on to false pretenses to see His true heart toward us. Do I let go of this tenth? Is it really necessary for me to give this piece to God? Is there really such a link between tithing and the more of God? Are my future blessings tied to my present giving? The only way you will truly know is to test God and see. Only if you try Him will your eyes be opened. He will show you a greater way. It doesn't work the other way, around, see and then try. I urge you to take the step of faith, try Him and see.

Bring a tenth of what you have been given into the storehouse. A storehouse is a building where goods are kept for future use. Why? So "that there may be meat in mine house" In other words, bring tithes into the storehouse that there may be maturity in My house..."Brothers and sisters, I could not address you as people who live by the Spirit but as people who are still worldly-mere infants in Christ I gave you milk, not solid food" (I Cor 3:1-3, NIV). Meat is solid food. Meat is for believers who have matured. Giving helps in the maturation process. There is nothing like giving. Giving is the evidence of true love. The greater the sacrifice, the greater display of love. There is no greater love than a man give up his life for a friend (John

15:13). The more giving a person is toward others the less selfish one is.

Giving trains us how to let go. We have to learn how to let go of what we have so we can receive "the next" from our Father. It builds our faith in our Father as a provider and sustainer. More specifically tithing is a consistent and current *practice* of our faith... like a doctor practices medicine or an attorney practices law. A tithe, a tenth, or the ten percent is the "works" that causes our faith to come alive. That means as God increases the portion He gives you so does the amount you give back to Him. Increase cannot manifest if you are still holding on saying, "mine, mine, mine!"

As a parent, I have a vision of the characteristics I desire to see develop in each of my children. One of my fears is they will get caught up in themselves, only thinking of what they want, unable to identify with the feelings of others, unable to see past their own wants and needs, too preoccupied with getting what they want to realize what God has already given to them so they can fill a need in others. Maturity can only be developed through the process of giving. You can evaluate your level of maturity by your willingness to let go of what by right belongs to you. How much are you willing to sacrifice for the big picture, the kingdom picture? Immaturity is a dead give away that you think too small, your focus is still self-centered. It's impossible to be immature *and* kingdom minded. Your giving is an investment in the kingdom of Heaven.

6

The Investor versus the Consumer

There is an innate desire in all of us to want more. In the same respect there is a certain level of discontentment in all of us. I see these two interdependent forces at work not only in my children but adults as well. No longer is the Nintendo DS good enough, the Nintendo 3DS-XL is better. The

Floodgates

iPhone 8 plus is not good enough, even though it still works well, I want the iPhone X. I want the new one, the better one. It is no help that we are constantly bombarded with ads, commercials, and programming appealing to our lusts of the flesh. I am no longer content with what I have, I want the next new and improved; the revolving door of desire and discontentment. I have made a conscious effort in raising my children to starve the selfish desires. When we go to the store we get what's on the list. I rarely allow them to deviate and add items according to their whims (and it must be on sale!). We are careful to buy them gifts for birthdays and Christmas, not too much in between. We try to instill a sense of work ethic and monetary responsibility, teaching them to work for the things they want and give appropriately to the Lord through tithe. But despite our efforts and my goal for them to be selfless servant givers. I find that there are times I feel as if I have missed it because they do not always display the qualities that I hoped for. For some reason despite our efforts they still find discontentment and they still want more! And if I am truly honest, I see the same tendencies in my own heart. At some point something new, grows old and stale. It was in my own self-reflection that the Lord showed me that these two qualities were placed in us by Him, our creator. Yes, I was also shocked to hear that these two qualities could be a good thing if directed toward our Heavenly Father. Be content with what you have but never grow content with where you are. Do enjoy earthly blessings, but feed your desire for more in Christ. Bottom line, there ought to be something in you that wants more, that is not content with the status quo. Something in you that dreams big and crazy! There has to be more than *this*.

Reflect on the parable of the talents. We see these two qualities at work, desire and discontentment. Two servants are rewarded and one servant is reprimanded.

The first servant was given five thousand dollars, which he invested and made a return of another five thousand dollars. The second servant was given two thousand dollars, which he also invested and made double on his return. Both servants were discontent with their status quo. They desired more. And no matter how much they were given they understood that there was still more. They were willing to take the risk to obtain more than what they had. In other words they saw the revelation of a giving father and could release what they had in their hands for more. They were willing to invest, allowing their investment to mature and grow.

> His master commended him: 'Good work! You did your job well. From now on be my partner'

> -Matt. 25:21, MSG

The investor understands the heart of God. The investor understands risk, faith, release, gains and losses, assets and liabilities, interest, maturity and wealth. An investor is someone who uses money to purchase products with the expectation of financial return. The Lord was pleased because they expected to receive, they expected increase. The Lord was so pleased that He promoted the two servants to be His partners! He is looking and desiring to promote those who prove faithful.

In contrast, there is the other servant, the consumer. The one that doesn't save or invest. The consumer is motivated by fear.

The servant given one thousand said, 'Master, I know you have high standards and hate careless ways, that you demand the best and make no allowances for error. I was afraid I might disappoint you, so I found a good hiding place and secured your money. Here it is, safe and sound down to the last cent.'

The master was furious. 'That's a terrible way to live! It's criminal to live cautiously like that! If you knew I was after the best, why did you do less than the least? The least you could have done would have been to invest the sum with the

The Investor versus the Consumer

bankers, where at least I would have gotten a little interest.

Take the thousand and give it to the one who risked the most. And get rid of this "play-it-safe" who won't go out on a limb. Throw him out into utter darkness.'

-Matt. 25:24-30, MSG

And we are back to fear and hiding ...again! He sounds just like Adam, "I was afraid, Lord, so I hid." The last servant is the consumer. Don't let fear be the reason you do not give tithe and offering. One of the most common statements I hear from non-tithing believers is that they do not trust what the leadership will do with the money. This is a fear tactic developed by the enemy to keep you from the blessing of the storehouse. The consumer is "an individual who buys products or services for personal use and not for manufacture or resale. A consumer is someone who makes decisions whether or not to purchase an item at the store, and someone who can be influenced by marketing and advertisements." A consumer buys things for personal use. They are easily influenced by outside sources and easily distracted. This person has difficulty seeing past what they want right now. This person has difficulty sacrificing the now for the later. The consumer thinks and says things like, "I'd rather enjoy the money now because I could die tomorrow."

There is nothing wrong with enjoying the things God has blessed us with on earth however, it is wrong if you are not investing in the kingdom of heaven. Remember without faith it is impossible to please God. We tithe unto God not unto man. Do not allow fear to dictate your obedience to God. The consumer is consumed with fear.

Ultimately, God will hold *you* responsible for your obedience. It won't matter what pastors or leaders "do" with the money, they will be accountable for any misuse of God's money. Again if you are concerned that the leaders of your church are misusing God's money, then prayerfully ask the Lord to lead you to a church where there is transparency and accountability. God will honor your obedience to *His* word. "test me now in this," says the LORD of hosts, "if I will not open you the windows of heaven."

7

The Windows of Heaven

Now let's begin our look at Malachi 3:8-10. "Bring ye all the tithes into the storehouse, that there may be meat in mine house, and prove me now herewith, saith the Lord of hosts, if I will not open you the windows of heaven, and pour you out a blessing, that there shall not be room to receive it." We have determined that it is necessary to bring the tithes into the storehouse in order for provision and worship to be re-established in our lives. Our focus will begin at verse 10. Read it aloud. "if I will not open **YOU**...the windows of heaven...and pour *you* out... That there shall not be room enough to receive."

In the Hebrew, "window" means sluice or floodgates, which traditionally are a wood or metal barrier sliding in grooves that are set in the sides of the waterway. They commonly control the water levels and flow rates in rivers and canals. They are also used in wastewater treatment plants and to recover minerals in mining operations and in watermills.

You are the window, *you* are the sluice, *you* are the floodgate...when *you* bring your tithe to the storehouse God opens *you*! Once God opens *you*, the Holy Spirit, the Living Water, can flow!

''Whoever believes in me, as Scripture has said, rivers of living water will flow from within them.' By this he meant the Spirit, whom those who believed in him were later to receive. Up to that time the Spirit had not been given, since Jesus had not yet been glorified" (John 7:38-39 NIV).

Floodgates

Once we are saved the Holy Spirit is given to us but as we develop and grow our gates open wider and wider. He can trust us with more when we prove to be faithful with the little. When we invest in the gift given to us there is increase. The Holy Spirit contains such power and force. This is why discipleship is critical in the body of Christ. We have to learn how to operate as floodgates. We have to manage and steward that which has been poured into us that we might pour into others. The focus must always be on God's original design and intent...an abundance of His presence and

His provision. The more we open up to God the more He opens to us. The Father restoring to us the provisions He had for us in the very beginning. The Holy Spirit allows us to see what God sees, call it forth, and then it manifests. When the maturation process is neglected we have untrained and undisciplined floodgates that will not operate properly. Which may explain a lot of the problems in the modern church today. In too many cases, many have not yet developed the character to minister effectively. Power without the nature of God developed and matured in your life is surely destined to pride and arrogance. Just ask the angel formally known as Lucifer.

Now how is it that you are a window *of heaven*? Let's take a look at the location of these windows, these sluices, these floodgates... they are located in heaven! This word heaven is translated as "high places" or "the highest heaven", referring to the dwelling place of God, the "third heaven," if you will. "But God, who is rich in mercy, out of the great love with which he loved us even when we were dead through our trespasses, made us alive together with Christ—by grace you have been saved— *and raised us up with him and seated us with him in the heavenly places in Christ Jesus,"* (Eph. 2:4-6 NRSV). We see in the book of Revelation 22:1 "the river of the water of life, as clear as crystal, flowing from the throne of God and of the Lamb." This river must be the living water, the Holy Spirit! Now you see why floodgates are necessary. All of that power flowing from the throne of God. No one on earth would be able to handle the fullness of all God's glory and power ...and live. So God in His infinite wisdom has made you and me a floodgate in heaven to pour into the earth.

Floodgates

Therefore, the floodgates are positioned in the heavenly places so that each may pour out according to their measure of faith. The more faith, the more flow. This is why "windows" is plural. Each believer is a window, each believer is a floodgate. This also is why we need to work together in unity. When we are all open we can flood the earth with His Spirit, His glory, and His power. As long as we are open, the Holy Spirit begins working in our lives, sanctifying us and revealing the treasures inside us. And thus begins the mining process.

Part Three

The Storehouse:
Revelation Revealed

"The LORD will open for you His good storehouse, the heavens, to give rain to your land in its season and to bless all the work of your hand; and you shall lend to many nations, but you shall not borrow.

Deuteronomy 28:12 NASB

The Storehouse: Revelation Revealed

As we begin to understand our kingdom position and role. Not only can we live in purpose and fulfillment, but as kingdom citizens we inherit kingdom benefits. Full access to the storehouse has been restored to us through the sacrifice of Jesus Christ. However, in order for us to take hold of the riches assigned to us, we must *see* that it has been made available. Only through revelation will the veil be lifted to see the treasure our Father has gifted to us. Revelation unlocks the treasure inside us and has great potential to influence many lives for the kingdom.

8

Discovering the Treasure

"How could she give me a "D"? That is not fair! "Well, I got a "B". I think it's because she likes me!"

These are the typical conversations of sixth graders I overheard in the halls following the distribution of report cards. Every time I would hear conversations of this nature, it made be cringe. It didn't even have to be a grade that reflected my class. It was the academic attitude. "She or he gave me..." Somehow students lacked the understanding of their ownership in earning the grade that appeared on their report card. After nine weeks of teaching, reteaching, tutoring, helping, encouraging, pleading, and begging, somehow it still alluded them that they had any authority in their academic career. A grade was something that just "happened" to them. It was like a grade was something teachers pulled out of thin air...poof...like magic. So I set in my mind, that I was going to do something about this! I decided for the next unit of study I would give my students the test. Yes, ...I did. At the beginning of the unit, I passed out a copy of the *actual* test. I told them, "This is the test. It is not a study guide, I'm not going to change anything; not a question, not any words, not any numbers. This is it." I looked out amongst a sea of confused faces, struggling to understand what I had given them. *Is she for real?* "Take five minutes to look through the first part of the test and right down any questions you do not understand." So each day I gave students time to look over the test and ask any questions they wanted during the first few minutes of class before we went into the lesson for the day. I didn't complete the actual test problem, but I would make up a similar problem. When test time came, I asked them to retrieve the test from their notebooks and begin. I was so excited! I just knew everyone would do well because I had given them everything they needed to be successful ...and more! I graded the test and sat down with each student. To my sadness, I would meet with several students about their grade and ask,

"Did you look at the test? Did you

study?"

..."No"

I never could understand why! Each student had the *same* opportunity but not each student *valued* the opportunity. They had something of value in their possession but did not see it. *Where do I go from here? I've given them everything*! I can imagine our Father shaking His head in frustration saying, "But I've given them everything!"

My students had exactly what they needed, and more, the entire time. Some of them endured hardships and frustrations they did not have to endure. They just had to trust my heart toward them and embrace my desire for each one of them to be successful. The treasure was there in their possession. Several of them just had to receive and utilize what had been given to them.

In the previous chapter we learned that windows is translated to mean a floodgate or sluice. A sluice is not only used to control flow rates in rivers, it is also used in the mining process. I was curious as to how this worked, so I Googled the process to see how minors use a sluice. First, a miner would get to a good place in the river where the current is just right, not too strong and not too weak. He sets up the sluice in the river. Then he carefully looks for a spot in the bedrock where there may be gold. He uses a shovel to get at the gravel and scoops the gravel into the sluice. The water runs over the dirt washing it out. But the gold stays behind.

So the Miner, Jesus Christ the son of God, takes the gravel, the filthy situations and circumstances of life, and scoops the gravel into you, the sluice. The Holy Spirit, the living water, runs over the dirt washing it out. This is the process known as sanctification. "As obedient children, do not conform to the evil desires you had when you lived in ignorance. But just as he who called you is holy, so be holy in all you do; for it is written: "Be holy, because I am holy" (1 Peter 1:14-16, NIV).

As we become more like Christ we regain the perspective of the Father. He draws us back to a place where abundance is stored. "I will give you hidden treasures, riches stored in secret places, so that you may know that I am the LORD, the God of Israel, who summons you by name" (Isaiah 45:3, NIV).

Let's review: We give tithe, God opens us up, the Holy Spirit, living waters, flows through *you,* a floodgate in heaven, where God raised us up and seated us with him so that he might show the immeasurable riches of his grace.

Remember that pin I mentioned at the end of chapter 4? God promised Abraham, "I will multiply you exceedingly." Now revisit the last part of Malachi 3:10, "if I will not open *you* the windows of heaven, and pour *you* out a blessing, that there shall not be room enough to receive it." But I'm going to move the comma. Repeat the following out loud, maybe several times: "if I will not open you the windows of heaven, *and pour you out, a blessing that there shall not be room enough to receive it.*"

Discovering the Treasure

For years I had this mental picture of an open window in heaven and God had this bucket full of blessings pouring it out. It's not so much that God is opening a window from heaven and blessing you...But God opens *you...you* are the window, you are the sluice, you are the floodgates, the river of the Holy Spirit is flowing in and through you! God will open you...the Holy Spirit sanctifies you and reveals the treasure in you. "so that in the ages to come he might show the *immeasurable riches* of his grace in kindness toward us in Christ Jesus. For by grace you have been saved through faith, and *this is not your own doing; it is the gift of God*— not the result of works, so that no one may boast" (Eph. 2:7, NASB). The same covenant blessing given to Abraham is available to you.

A sluice is a tool that is necessary because we can't handle *all* of the glory of God-that's why it is a gradual release. As we grow and mature, giving God what is His, He opens us up. Which "us" does he open?... the one seated in heavenly places the one seated in Christ so that the gift of God, the Holy Spirit can flow through you--collecting the immeasurable riches of his grace. The treasure in you is so great that there shall not be room enough to receive it!

In John 4:10-14 NASB, Jesus answered and said to her, "If you knew the gift of God, and who it is who says to you, 'Give Me a drink,' you would have asked Him, and He would have given you living water." She said to Him, "Sir, You have nothing to draw with and the well is deep; where then do You get that living water? You are not greater than our father Jacob, are You, who gave us the well, and drank of it himself and his sons and his cattle?" Jesus answered and said to her, "Everyone who drinks of this water will thirst again; but whoever drinks of the water that I will give him shall never thirst; but the water that I will give him will become in him a well of water springing up to eternal life." Then Jesus says "God is spirit and those who worship Him must worship in spirit and truth" God makes restoration through the person of the Holy Spirit.

Now since we have established what you are and where you are, we are going to back up to focus on Malachi 3 verse 8, "Will a man rob God? Yet ye have robbed me. But ye say, Wherein have we robbed thee? *How* do *we* rob God? Robbery is to take something illegally by using force or a threat of force. I have heard many preachers describe the difference between robbery and stealing. Robbery is someone taking something that belongs to you right in front of your face, many times by force or intimidation. Stealing is sneaky, those who steal take what belongs to you behind your back, or while you're not home or paying attention. This is why God says you *rob* me, not you steal from me. Remember where you are? Remember where God raised you up in Christ? You are seated in the heavenly realm, right in the face of God! God has given you the gift of the Holy Spirit, a gift of grace, a gift of immeasurable riches, yet because you disobey, your sluice, your floodgates remain closed, no water is flowing. That is why people remain spiritually dry- the water - living water is in you but the living water is restricted by a dam of disobedience. This is the curse: having the potential of God's presence but never having access, hearing the word but never being a doer, knowing the word but never having revelation.

Believers who do not consistently tithe are subject to have little or shallow revelation.

> These things God has revealed to us by his Spirit. The Spirit searches all things even the deep things of God" For who knows a person's thoughts except their own spirit within them? In the same way no one knows the thoughts of God *except* the Spirit of God. What we have received is not the spirit of the world, but the spirit who is from God so that *we* may understand what God has freely given

us...The person without the spirit does not accept the things that come from the spirit of God but considers them foolishness, and cannot under-stand them because they are discerned only through the Spirit.

-1 Cor. 2:10-12,14, NIV

(Italics added for emphasis)

This is why a non-tither will have shallow revelation, shallow water, shallow spirit. Therefore what God has already given to him, he will not see; what God has already said to him he will not hear. In Ephesians 3:17-20, Apostle Paul prays for the believers, desiring them to realize what they have in

99

Christ through the Holy Spirit, praying that their eyes would be opened to see what they already have.

> asking God, the glorious Father of our Lord Jesus Christ, to give you spiritual wisdom and insight so that you might grow in your knowledge of God. I pray that your hearts will be flooded with light so that you can understand the confident hope he has given to those he called—his holy people who are his rich and glorious inheritance. I also pray that you will understand the incredible

greatness of God's power for us who believe him. This is the same mighty power that raised Christ from the dead and seated him in the place of honor at God's right hand in the heavenly realms.

- Ephesians 3:17-20, PAS

The gifts and treasures are there but without the veil being lifted he cannot receive what he does not see. We know nothing except the Spirit reveal it to us. "However, it is written: what no eye has seen, what no ear has heard, and what no human mind has conceived the things of God has prepared for those who love Him, These things God has revealed to us by his

Spirit" (1 Cor. 2:9-14, NIV). The things God has prepared for us, given us, stored up for us...have to be revealed by the Spirit. If the Spirit doesn't reveal them, even the blessings already in our possession we won't see. Even though they are right in front of our face. The storehouse, just like in Eden, is full of treasures and riches that exceed the needs of man. If you can receive what God has revealed to you, you will live in overflow.

9

The Overflow

Not too long ago some women and I were praying for a woman and as we prayed the Lord showed me a bathtub filling up with water. The faucet continued to run and the water began to spill over and flood the floor. This vision of overflow stayed with me. It is what He desires to do in all of our lives. He desires to fill us with

Floodgates

His Spirit and spill over flooding the earth.

In the last part of Malachi 3:10 God says, "pour you out, …a blessing that there shall not be room enough to receive it." The storehouse is filled with purposes, giftings, blessings and benefits. These are the treasures we can access if we walk in obedience to God's word and allow the Holy Spirit to cleanse us and reveal to us the treasures God has placed in us.

Honor the Lord with your wealth, with the firstfruits of all your crops; then your barns will be filled to overflowing, and your vats will brim over with new wine.

-Prov. 3:9-10, NIV

I love this! Not only does the Holy Spirit exemplify living water but new wine. Remember, "Do not get drunk on wine, which leads to debauchery. Instead, be filled with the Spirit," (Eph. 5:18, NIV). I have often wondered why Jesus' very first miracle, would be to turn water to wine.

> Now there were six stone waterpots set there for the Jewish custom of purification, containing twenty or thirty gallons each. Jesus said to them, "Fill the waterpots with

water." So they filled them up to the brim.

The number six in the bible represents man's weakness or man's imperfection. It is also believed according to Jewish tradition, the pots were there to be used for "purification." These water pots were filled with water to symbolize man's need to be purified or cleansed from weaknesses and imperfections caused by sin. This process was necessary before attempting to enter into the presence of God.

The Overflow

Before the wedding, Jesus had just completed forty days of fasting in the wilderness, resisting every temptation, rebuking Satan and overcoming the very roots of every human weakness. He came to establish our righteousness, and solidify our cleanliness through Him. He set sanctification in motion, making holiness and godliness possible. So it is divinely meticulous that for Jesus' first miracle, He takes these six waterpots full of water intended to purify, intended for cleansing and turns the water to wine... new wine. Our Father sent His son to redirect our focus. Before Jesus, the focus was on getting clean and staying clean. But this "New Wine" shows us a more excellent way. We have the assurance that we have been made clean. It is done, once and for all. Now we are free to shift our focus to His influence. Water cleanses, but Wine *influences*.

> and the master of the banquet tasted the water that had been turned into wine. He did not realize where it had come from, though the servants who had drawn the water knew. Then he called the bridegroom aside and said, "Everyone brings out the choice wine

first and then the cheaper wine after the guests have had too much to drink; but you have saved the best till now."

-John 2:10, NIV

Yes, the Lord loves to save the best for last! This first miracle, sign, wonder, is the inauguration of the Holy Spirit, an abundance of His Spirit, bringing us back to our Father's perspective and love. Once you allow the Holy Spirit to cleanse you of your weakness and imperfections, then He influences you...and *you* become the influential blessing that there is not room enough to receive. Here is the last part of the story, "This beginning of His signs Jesus did in Cana of Galilee, and manifested His glory, and His disciples believed in Him" (John 2:11, NASB). Look at the influence He had on the people of Cana, the servants, the master of the banquet, the bridegroom, His mother and His disciples. Revelation through the power of the Holy Spirit uncovers, cleanses and influences you so that we can re-unite with our Creator and we can again walk in provision and worship. In this walk His glory is manifested in our lives.

Conclusion

Therefore looking at Malachi 3:8-10, top down, from a heavenly perspective; it may read something like this:

Take a portion of the gifts I've given to you and bring it to the building that will store the goods for future use, this is so that maturity will develop in my house. Now test my word. As you mature, see if I will not open you, the sluice, the floodgates; as you are seated in heavenly places with Christ. From this heavenly position I will pour *You* out into the earth. Now through the revelation of the Holy Spirit, you can see the treasure inside you and the blessings of overflow that God has already prepared and stored for you in such an unimaginable way that you will bless and influence others.

Notes

Chapter 1

The Original Design and Intent

1. Merriam-Webster Dictionary, s.v., "formless," https://www.merriam-webster.com/dictionary/formless (accessed April 20, 2017).

2. BibleGateway,https://www.biblegateway.com/passage/search=Genesi1&version=KJV (accessed April 20, 2017

3. **Chapter 2**

The Fellowship of the Father

and His Beloved

1. Dictionary.com, s.v., "beloved," http://www.dictionary.com/browse / beloved (accessed April 20, 2017).

Chapter 3

The Struggle

1. BibleHub.com, s.v., "acknowledge," http://biblehub.com/topical/a/ acknowledge.htm (accessed July 23, 2017)

Chapter 4

A Covenant Blessing

1. BibleGateway,https://www.biblegate way. com/passage/ search= Ephesians %203:9-11&version=NLT, (accessed September 30, 2017).

Chapter 5

The Maturation Process

1. Financial Peace University, www
   fpucentral.com (accessed
   Nov ember 23, 2017).

Chapter 6

The Investor versus the Consumer

1. Investorwords.com, s.v., "investor,"
   http://www.investorwords.com /
   2630/investor.html#ixzz4p5f1TkUp,
   (accessed August 7, 2017).

2. Investorwords.com, s.v. "consumer,"
   http://www.investorwords.com/1055
   /consumer.html#ixzz4psfNNu3L,
   accessed August 15, 2017).

3. Biblegateway.com,https://www.bible
   gateway.com/passage/?
   search=Matthew+25%3A14-
   30&version=MSG, (accessed July 28,

2017).

Chapter 7

The Windows of Heaven

1. James Strong, s.v., "window," The New Strong's Expanded Exhaustive Concordance of the Bible Red-Letter Edition, (TN: Thomas Nelson Publishers, 2003).

2. Wikipedia.org, s.v., "sluice," https://en.wikipedia.org/wiki/Sluice (accessed April 14, 2017).

3. James Strong, s.v., "heaven," The New Strong's Expanded Exhaustive Concordance of the Bible Red-Letter Edition, (TN: Thomas Nelson Publishers, 2003).

Chapter 8

Discovering the Treasure

1. Wikipedia.org, s.v., "sluice,"

https://en.wikipedia.org/wiki/Sluice
(accessed April 14, 2017).

2. freedictionary.com, s.v., "robbery,"
   http://legaldictionary.thefree.diction
   ary.com/robbery (accessed June 24,
   2017).

3. Merriam-Webster.com, s.v.,
   "stealing,"https://www.merriam-
   webster.com/ thesaurus/stealing
   (accessed June 24, 2017).

4. Biblehub.com, s.v., "acknowledge"
   http://biblehub.com/topical/a/Ackn
   owledge.htm (June 24, 2017).

About the Author

ELISABETH JOHNSON is a full-time wife and mother of four. Growing up as a PK, pastor's kid, she has served as a leader in ministry nearly 15 years, in the areas of christian education and intercession; and is a founding member of New Beginnings Christian Church. She committed her early career to public education, earning her B.S. and Masters in Elementary Education and National Board Certification in Early Adolescents Mathematics. In 2013 she was a semi-finalist for Alabama State Teacher of the Year. Currently she is an education consultant with a local university.

Elisabeth embraces her calling as a prophetic intercessor and serves as an associate minister at her church. She desires to transform the world around her as she is being transformed, one sentence at a time.

Connect and Share

I would love to hear from you! Write me at:

theflipsiderevealed@gmail.com

or stop by my website:

www.theflipsiderevealed.com

If you were challenged and encouraged after reading this book, please consider sharing a review on Amazon or sharing on your favorite social media platform.

Check out these resources!

Floodgates: Discovering the Treasure within You Workbook

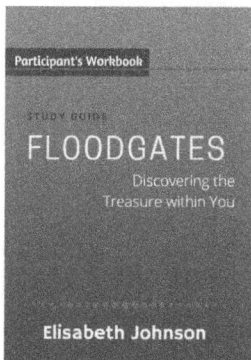

Participant's Workbook

STUDY GUIDE

FLOODGATES

Discovering the
Treasure within You

Elisabeth Johnson

This online workbook is a great resource to deepen your understanding. It includes discussion questions, activities that can be used for individual or small group study. Although the workbook is a comprehensive study that can be used independently, it is most beneficial when used alongside the book *Floodgates*.

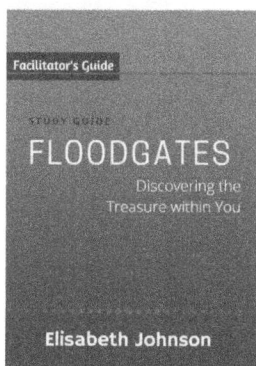

Facilitator's Guide

STUDY GUIDE

FLOODGATES

Discovering the
Treasure within You

Elisabeth Johnson

Floodgates: Discovering the Treasure within You Facilitator's Guide

The facilitator's guide contains extra notes, insight, and suggestions for a small group facilitator.

Available at
www.theflipsiderevealed.com

www.ingramcontent.com/pod-product-compliance
Lightning Source LLC
Chambersburg PA
CBHW03151604026
42445CB00009B/260